My Journey Out of Darkness

A Poetry Collection

Christopher Zee Chartrand

A friend is someone who not only wishes

you well on a journey, but instead says

"wake me up when we get there."

Dedication

I dedicate this collection of poems and thoughts to my eldest daughter, editor, and friend, Trinity. Without her ongoing support and dedication, this effort would not have come to fruition.

It's an amazing moment when a father recognizes their offspring has surpassed them. How does such an amazing instance of beauty occur? How can such joy be contained and held? I stand in wonder and awe.

Trinity, I will never obtain the words to express my gratitude to you fully - and even more lagging - my ability and creativity to articulate the depth of love I have for you.

Contents

Introduction

This effort was started as a personal quest to improve mental health and stability. Initially, I just started writing blurbs and quotes, singular thoughts. Soon I found the slightly longer poetic form of writing to be more appealing, rewarding and helpful. With the appropriate amount of effort, I discovered that I could investigate my thoughts and feelings independently and at my own pace.

The journey aspect of the poetry was not intended but, in hindsight, seems rather an obvious progression. Although not directly correlated, the negative, more traumatic poetry naturally came first. As I processed those emotions and moved through and eventually past them, the more growth-related and hopeful poetry naturally sprang forth.

The loss and love section is a recurring theme. Even though I am happily single, I still find value in honestly contemplating my historical thoughts and recognizing my ongoing related traumas and feelings.

I hope that some of my insights may help you process your emotions and improve your well-being and, in rare cases, elucidate and describe in words what you may have been feeling for some time but were unable to articulate fully.

Finally, a special thanks to my friends and family who (anonymously) contributed such amazing original artwork to this passion project. I am truly blessed to have such gifted and talented people like you in my life!

Foreword

It can be said that poetry is the most personal approach to sharing perspectives. Chris does not disappoint as he shares his life experiences in this collection of writings, "My Journey Out of Darkness."

Beginning at a very dark time of his life, the agony of being a victimized, vulnerable child starts this journey. There is only one way to go from such a start. Chris shares his complex life struggles through questioning and learning to understand and acknowledge his relationships, failures and successes. It is a bumpy road.

During his reflections on psilocybin use, I found myself cheering and giggling at the insights and progress Chris described. His musings on each of his many experiences were troubled, thoughtful and most certainly insightful. An amazing read!

Future readers will find themselves wishing Chris joy, happiness and dancing on his continuing journey to the light.

- Brenda Baker

A Time for Infancy

But it is new every time.

I am a strong believer in taking personal responsibility for personal actions[1]. However, how much responsibility can a completely vulnerable child achieve prior to any self-actualization? In this regard, my personal journey starts in childhood with a few harms and many omissions. Your journey may begin elsewhere, although all too commonly, trauma and pain are often most felt at a young age when full hope and guidance are placed in those in whom you are taught to trust the most for raw safety.

In my view, some of these writings are the most painful to write and read, but early on offered me great insight into where a lot of my adult deficiencies were possibly sourced from. Getting to the heart of the issue, dissecting, and understanding are stages in my pursuit of mental health wellness.

---

[1] Oddly, in contrast to my lack of belief that free will exists (for various reasons, I will not delve into it here). I openly acknowledge that I must continue my life pretending that free will does exist.

Tears of the Lonely Child

Normalising the incidence

When a child questions their worth

When a child seeks

But does not find

Any reason to continue

Represents a magnitude of sadness

That is difficult to articulate

As an adult, I think in terms of

Responsibility and confidence

Should we judge the child

For having an innocent ignorance of such things?

For lacking even the words

To articulate one's feelings?

"Why didn't you come to me!"

"Why didn't you tell me!"

The child could not, can not

Self-hatred and fear

Is all the child knows

And those are communicated with tears

Quiet and alone

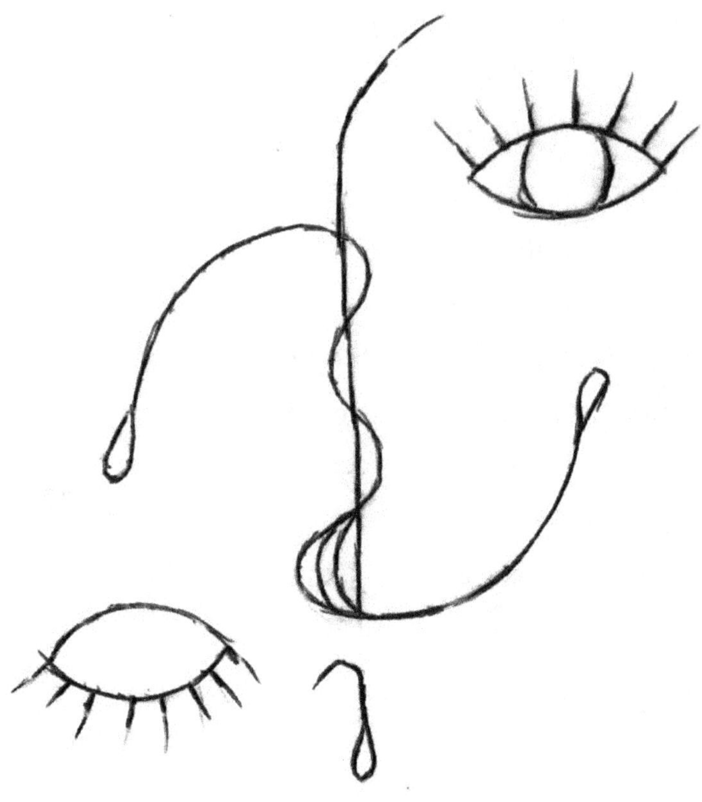

Alone on the Ocean

I can see now

That I have never felt safe

This motivating factor

Is negated by the long-term

Stress-induced destruction

Security is an illusion

If you think you possess it

Be ever so grateful

For this veil of ignorance

I accept the true nature of the horror

The only sense of loss I have left

Is that even as a child

I experienced no comfort

There was never a time of delusion

Can one mourn the loss

Of something we never had?

Quiet and Alone

Mourn the child

Who could not be

Was not permitted to feel

Lived only for others

Hide those feelings!

Stifle those thoughts!

Turn ever more inwards

Cry alone

But do so ever so quietly

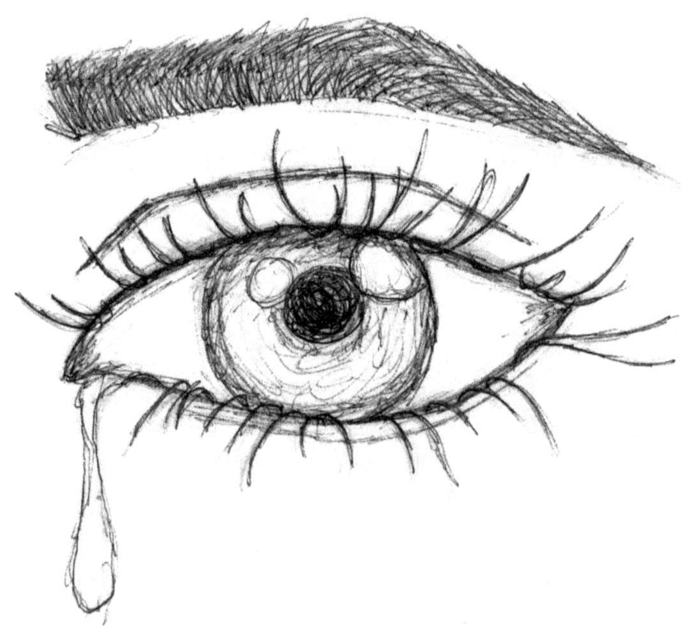

Lost Potential

What sort of person

Causes such harm to a child?

Deception, indoctrination

Is your ignorance and self-delusion

Enough to garner forgiveness?

I am not convinced

For the simple truth of the matter

Is life is simply too short

The fundamental change

To the young, malleable mind

Outlasts the blip of a life

This infinitely thin slice of eternity

The responsibility was yours

And your failure was complete

Weep for the Loss

Dig deep

Cry unabashedly

Is the memory of the pain enough?

A sprinkling of potential future calamity

Should wrench me over the threshold

Oh, sweet relief

When the dam breaks

The pressure is released

Weep for the loss

Weep for what could have been

The Gift

Who did the child want to be?

Shackled and hidden away

Living only for others

A true polymorph

The memories of terror and insecurity

Are frighteningly vivid

But what little you have left to give

Give only to those who should have noticed

A Time for Despair

I cried from the memory of the pain.

Trauma is something we all have or will most likely experience at some point, to various degrees of severity. I find it quite fulfilling and therapeutic to consider my past traumas, and more than once have discovered interesting threads that help me long after writing about them. I consider, at one point, as I am contemplating my past neglect, if it is required to process this pain to get past it - I have no education in these matters and am still unsure of the answer.

As you read, process and contemplate this pain with me, please keep in good cheer - these thoughts and feelings represent an early step in a long journey - it can only get better from here!

Recovery of the Broken

Recovering from trauma

Is an idea pushed

By those who have not been

Completely shattered

As for the rest of us

The best we can hope for

Is a mangled, disfigured perception

Of who we once were

Dreams, hope and joy

Are options only for the other

Cycles

Consider pain

A teachable moment?

Only if you learn from it

Is life just pain?

I visualise infinite cycles

The goddess of light knows

But who knows her?

Can we? Should we? Do we even want to?

Would the answer lead to even greater depths of pain?

Fucking cyclic bullshit

Is pain the motivation or the outcome?

Perhaps, the engine of the world

Self-Forgiveness

I seem to be limited

By a threshold of self-doubt

A core hatred of my definition

I would never allow this

To exist in the ones I love

For their hearts are pure

Others' flaws offer friction in which to cling

I see only motive

Never individual mistakes

Is my motivation any less pure?

I recognize my brokenness

My key failings

Self-forgiveness

Remains ever so elusive

Encompassing Darkness

My mask is getting heavy now

The raw truth is

I just don't give a fuck

What more do I have to lose?

How much further can I fall?

The distinction is much more

Then a simple matter of degree

To stand back and observe

Society at its worst

To recognize its path

Is destined for destruction

Empathy, vulnerability, sacrifice

These concepts are pure fantasy

Unknown, lost, foreign

What a badge of honour

To demonstrate such qualities

And to be fully rejected

By those who have forgotten

She Will Eventually Heal

I am afraid

The type of horror

That awakens you in the night

A visceral, guttural based feeling

I recognize my limited successes

I acknowledge my privilege and position

I am thankful every day

Still, I remain afraid

I mourn for our species

Even as I am thankful

That Gaia[2] will soon have a chance

To heal from our inflicted scars

On a more human timeline

The enumeration of pending doom possibilities

Is both well fleshed out and inevitable

---

[2] To learn more: https://en.wikipedia.org/wiki/Gaia_hypothesis

Shorter still, I can see

With ever-increasing clarity

The vapidness, the very illusion

Of the house of cards we call "society"

Go back to sleep

Dream of hope, fables and love

Dreams are the only refuge that remains

Dark Clarity

If you were looking for a happy ending

Look elsewhere

In my dark place

Two things have become clear

In the spirit of caring for others

My best, the only path forward

Is to remove myself from the equation

Even more profound an idea

Is the inescapable truth

That in cosmic time

And Cartesian planes

Nothing at all matters

To derive any meaning

You must focus small, local

Thinking at any scale

Leads only to demise

Monday Blues

My constant inability

To self diagnose

Reminds me of a plot device

In a failed movie

Perhaps it is just really complex

A convergence of multiple threads

But just as likely

I fear it is obvious

Blindingly simple and fundamental

I seek deep meaning

Complex chains and triggers

The sad conclusion

After moderate effort applied

Is I hate fucking Mondays

The Finish Line

I long for the race to be over

To coast calmly to the finish line

To be welcomed and comforted by adoring fans

But the road ahead has many coils

I can not yet see the end

I see the signs of progress

The slow build up of pain and acid is ever-present

But no indicator of distance communicated

I am alone

The very thought

That there may be many miles to go

Consumes me with dread

The race will eventually end

I envy those who have reached that goal

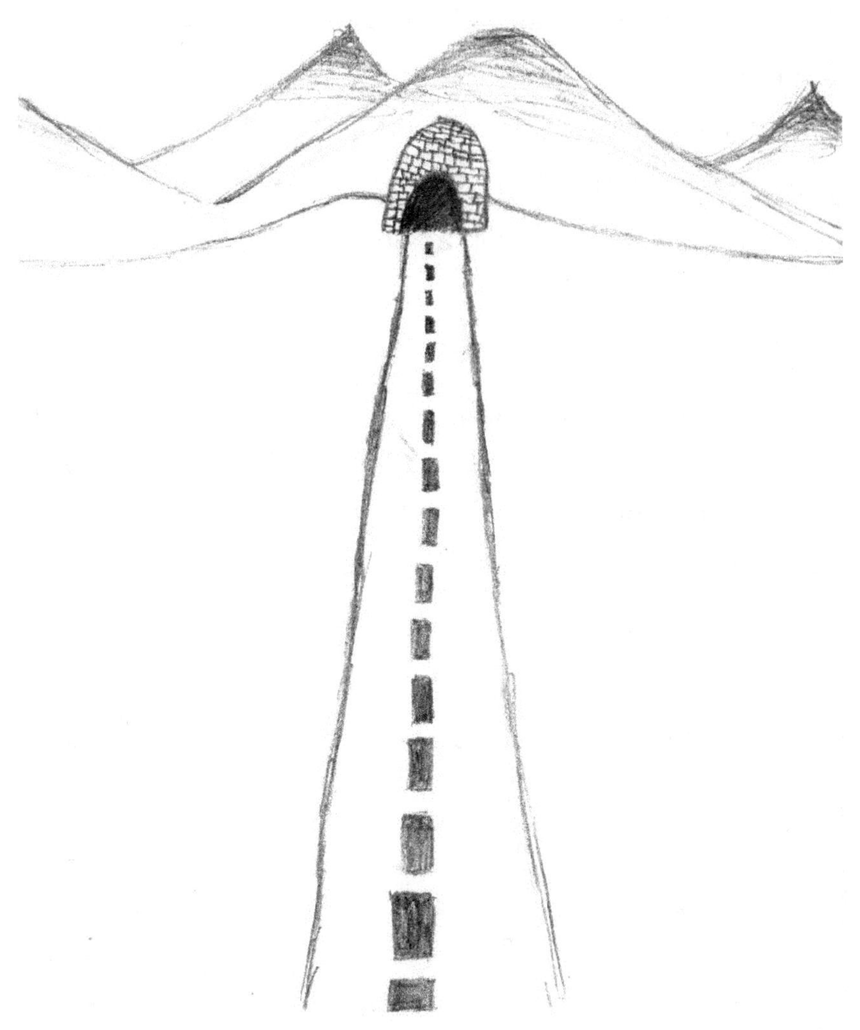

Recurring Shame

Don't judge me too harshly

For wanting to give up

With such a sequence of failures

I am open to accept

The convergence centres on me

The resilience to get up

After being knocked down again

Is considered by many

To be the greatest of virtues

Knowing when to quit

When to throw in the towel

Is more frequently

The rational choice

Doing the maths

The harsh reality is reflected

Rare events happen all the time

The decision when to fold

Is pushed to another day

Darkness Distinguished

A healthy state

A general well being

Cannot be distinguished

From the completely broken - the numb

Is the very notion

The very thought

Not all the proof you need?

What Darkness Remains

What I believe

What I can back up with evidence

Shocks me to the core

Even more terrifying

By an order of magnitude or greater

Lies in the vast void of ignorance

That dwarfs what we think we know

What darkness, what horrors

Lie in wait in those dark shadows?

I can almost hear you retort

Of the solutions, hopes and dreams

That may also reside in the ignorance

If these possibilities come to pass

I will, with jubilation, admit my folly

But if history has taught me anything

It is in the inevitableness of demise

Obvious Insights

I am broken

You may not know it

But I am

You are broken

You may not know it

But you are

Morning Tea

Like my morning tea

So is a life

Initially burning with the flame of desire and hope

Giving rise to the day's potential

Simply fades with time

The analogy remains poignant

For I am not yet alone

There are threads

They are weak

And they are few

But I suppose as long as any thread remains

I shall remain also

I can endure the lukewarm phase

The memory of the pure potency

Is enough to keep the taste alive

Eventually, naturally and inevitably

The energy dissipates, and coolness is achieved

Now the disgust overwhelms me

The choice to waste and dump

Becomes a stark and valid option

I consider the unitary flow of entropy

However, only applying to an isolated system[3]

---

[3] This important part of the second law of thermodynamics is so often overlooked or misquoted and misunderstood, a real pet peeve of mine!

The Winning Ticket

The myth of happiness with another

Is propagated by those

Statistically unlikely few

Who have stumbled blindly

On this cosmic lottery

Hope is only preached

By those with a bias toward its success

The rest of us - the majority

Recognize with a tear

That hope is the exception

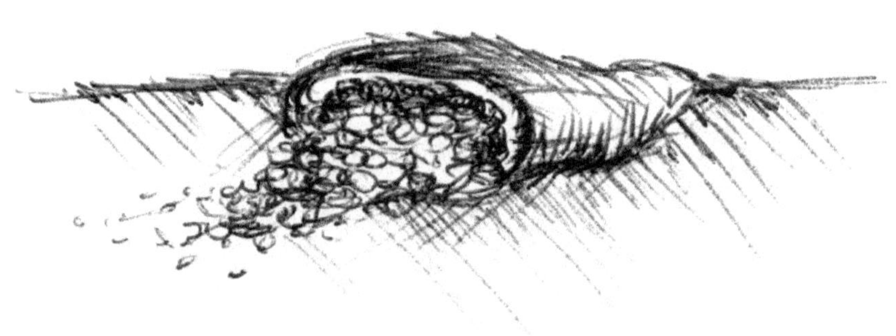

A Time for Love

Is love more like a song or a dance?

I have loved and lost, and the final tally of cost versus rewards is yet to be determined. Still, I am inclined to be thankful overall for the majority of the opportunities I have had to share my life with another special person. I am a strong believer that ultimate joy can only be found by expressing true authenticity with those you love[4] - I wish for you to know and put into practice this subtle truth - the world could certainly use a strong dose of authenticity in today's meandering society.

Love is almost synonymous with being human, in my opinion. Thus it is not surprising that a large portion of my mental fortitude is spent processing these past, current and potential future feelings. Today as I stand back and consider past relationships, hurts, and joy, I am very aware not to glorify the memories and mix a healthy dose of logic with the obvious feelings that stem from fully integrating with another.

---

[4] Sincere educational thanks to
https://en.wikipedia.org/wiki/Bren%C3%A9_Brown

Astronomical

How, how can this be?

The emotional depth

The astronomical odds

Events like this

Mathematically should not occur

But here you are - standing before me

Time has no meaning

Distance irrelevant

All the past hurt, the pain

Is not even a drop in the sea

Compared to my love for you

Love's Momentum

I still love you

Why so shocked?

Perhaps it is a degree of definition

But my love is not so fleeting

It has both mass and kinetics

Thus it remains powerful

A perpetual force

Not to be trifled with

I am not denying the harm

I am not ignorant of our pain

These are just dents

Mere chinks in the armour

One day it may cease

But today, my love

It endures

Love's Reflection

As the moon offers only reflection

My radiance

Represents only a reflection of your beauty

I have nothing more to give

Comfort and care for you

But the source

The true power

Was always, will always

Lie within you

My state of non-being

My dedication to vulnerability

Seems so attractive, so inviting

But only in contrast

To the norm of selfishness

I am not so unique

I just am

Shared Pain

Tell me everything about your pain

Hold nothing in check

Your tears

Your agony

Your greatest loss

In this, we will bond

Where there is now only a void

Was once filled and complete

The shape of your hole is telling

We are all broken

Let us never forget

Together

Inevitable Change and Potentials

Your skin was soft to the touch

Has it become less so over the years?

Your joy and focus burst forth

Do you still laugh unabashedly?

Your fear of self-reflection was vivid

Have you faced off against your demons?

Change is a constant

Surviving even our mortality, our humanity

This much is true

But we can choose to feed the blaze

Or stifle its combustion

What quality of fuel have you used

To kindle your fire of progress?

I hope to learn your light rages

And has settled to a steady slow burn

Let the rising embers of passion

Guide your way to a better future

I knew you once - I loved you then

Who have you become

And does that love remain?

Could our warmth burn as one again?

Rekindling the flames of passion and hope?

Or would one consume the other

Extinguishing the other's potential?

Is the value of this mystery

More so than learning a dismal truth?

Breakfast by Candlelight

All I want

Is all of you

Is it too much to ask

To lay forever in your arms?

Permanence of desire

Eternal pleasure, joy

The thoughts of you overwhelm me

Drown me in your love

My submission to you

Is complete and everlasting

The Dream

Come to me, oh dark one

My arms are open and waiting

You may not recognize it yet

But I am the one

Only together are we each made whole

I have travelled far

Your journey has just begun

From now on, our paths will be shared

This all feels like a dream

And it most certainly is

The question of importance is

Will you share the delusion with me?

Authentic Confessions

My heart aches again

I thought the time of sharp pain had ended

But the memory of you

Opens up old wounds

Would being with you end the torment?

Or restart the cycle of distress?

The pain of your loss

The gaping hole that was created

Has yet to heal

I expect can never, will never heal

On this day, however

After so much time has passed

I sit in wonder

At how you consume my thoughts

Healthy or not

Today I accept, I dare confess

My enduring love for you

The Book of Love

If my time with you

Was just a chapter in my book

A local maximum[5] in my story arc

I accept it with pleasure

New chapters have now been penned

Adventures, joys, pain

All dry ink on the page

But as the remaining empty pages

Are fewer than the completed ones

I can not help to think

If there will be another chapter

Starring you

---

[5] Also known as the "First Derivative Test" in calculus.

Let Her Go Free

Still no word from you

On this frosty spring morning

As you moved forward

I stand still

I am perplexed by the fact

That I am neither sad nor upset

I assume you chose to improve your position

Due to my love, my adoration

This brings me great joy

You were never mine

I never wished to own or control you

When I said I want the best for you

It was simply a statement of fact

I cannot be injured any further

It is not due to shielding

But because my destruction has long been completed

Soar, fly higher

I remain present, grounded

Puzzle Pieces

I present my brokenness

If you are able, share your pain in return

Perhaps in time

We can form a mosaic

Something more, something beautiful

From the shards of our past hurts

Others may criticise our design

But our judgements

Are the sole arbiters

I already accept

Our portrait may shatter again

But never again will I be alone

Never again will you be alone

Our pieces are mingled forever

You are a part of me now

Your pain adds a richness

For which I will always be grateful

Questioning the Past

The breaking point

Seems so clear

In the moment

Justifications are ever-present

Self-preservation takes over

But as time passes

I question the logic

I question everything

Could I have borne the weight

Has my patience just worn thin?

Hard boundaries, hard rules

Simply do not apply

To you, my love

Last Night

Fly away with me, my love

I long to reach great heights

Without even leaving the ground

To be in your presence

Defines my ecstasy

I had you last night in my dream

I wish to blur those lines

Dreams becoming reality

Reality manifesting as dreams

Was your dream oh so vivid?

Can you make the leap into reality?

I wait with an open embrace

Let me tend to your wounds

Tenderly press my lips to your scars

Have you forgotten I already know each mark?

You see blemishes, I see eternal love

Whatever you calculate my longing for you

You grossly underestimate

I seek you again in slumber

Eternal Refuge

Do you know

That I am a place of refuge?

Come to me

In your time of need

No matter who you are with

No matter where you have been

I remain

My very purpose is you

A shelter is but a taste

I offer so much more

And request so little

Forever Satiated

If you ever took pleasure

In being loved by me

Revel in the fact

That my love does not cease

I am fed

By the memory of you

A Time for Loss

This world is not well suited for those who feel too deep.

As often as I have had the distinct pleasure of knowing love, I have also experienced a corresponding loss. I do not announce this with a request for condolence or in a self-deprecation manner, simply an acknowledgement that for the vast majority of us, the score of love found versus loved lost is either tied or at most differs by one - I am simply in a state of equality at this moment.

The feeling of loss represents an important emotional state to process on the road to full self-recovery, as guilt, shame and regret have no part in one that desires to achieve wholeness and feelings of self-worth.

It took me a long time to realise and come to terms with the fact that I do have intrinsic value, and as soon as this void was acknowledged and dealt with[6], dealing with loss became a much easier and more manageable task.

---

[6] With a great deal of professional help, I might add. My eternal gratitude to Judith Wiley of Brantford, Ontario, who has been a guiding light for over ten years now in my healing process. http://www.judith-wiley.ca/

Loving the Thing that Hurts You

I found the love of my life

She didn't[7]

The story is as old as time

But the brutalness of it

Burns like a fresh wound

The ability of one to take

Will always surpass

Your ability to give

Perhaps I should be thankful

To my deep-seated monkey brain

For the instinct and desire to continue

Albeit in a disfigured and distorted state

Is an existence nonetheless

---

[7] Making every effort to avoid plagiarism, I first read some variation of this phrase years ago when searching for something like "Short sad stories." I made efforts to recognize and credit the original author, but it appears this has been lost over time or always was simply anonymous.

Lasting Effects

Where did joy go?

When did it become so elusive?

Track back in time

Was it all to do with you?

It is just so hard to feel

It is just so hard to tell

With a you shaped hole

In my chest

It's more than a scar

It defines my very being

My very nature clings to the pain

Final Wishes

I withhold the worst parts

I fear the very weight of it

Would crush you

I seek neither atonement nor assistance

The pain is mine and mine alone

I know I am loved

I love you in return

It is for this very reason

I cannot let you penetrate the veil[8]

The false harmony

The feigned laughter

Is the highest pinnacle

I can hope to reach

My whole heart-felt hope for you

Is for you to journey forward

To an unforeseen higher summit still unseen

Leave my death behind

And carry on

-----

[8] Over time and experience, I have learned the desire to share one's full authenticity needs to be balanced by restricting it to those who deserve it.

Shattered

How can my heart be broken

When it is already shattered?

I beat you to the punch

Oh, loves inevitable demise

I don't seek the numbness, the collapse

It just simply is

For this, I apologise

I extend my condolences

To the impending death

Yet I remain grateful

For your sincere efforts

To work with, to form

What I have left to offer

I tell you upfront

I will never be whole again

Moving On

I looked to you

To find pure joy

For a time, there was laughter

Intimate contemplation followed

But then you moved on

While still being here

The absent present is brutal

Now I look to you

No longer

The Missing

The void of you

The absence of your scent

The emptiness of not gently touching

Not sharing our daily troubles

The missing is pain

The Mystery

The dilemma of desire

Why is it so oft

That the ones we desire

Reject us outright?

Those who desire us

Are discarded without malice

The dream of mutual love

In only a distant fantasy

The notion of self-love

And its loftier twin hatred

Is certainly a piece of the puzzle

For the pieces to fit properly

To form a beautiful portrait

Requires knowledge and acceptance

Of one's self

Thus I remain alone

The Curse

The real curse

Is the fog of memory

Piercing passion

The clarity of your form

Is delegated to mere haze

Each bead of sweat

Fueled by primal lust

Is not just a construct

Of my ageing mind

Was it even real?

It must have been

For the vanity of my creativity

Has not yet reached such heights

What Remains

The pain is not from being broken

It is from remaining

What can you do with the pieces?

Some bright, sharp-edged ones

Others dull and weathered

I am a burden

Not a gift

Yet I contemplate the exchange

To you - the one who broke me

Root Causes

I didn't leave you because of your crimes

Your active and willful causation of pain

For I forgave you

Entirely and without discussion

In the early morning dawn

For this is how I love

Your inability to recognize

These gifts of love, forgiveness

Speaks to a deeper flaw

I have carried that burden before

I have carried that burden long enough

I refuse to carry it again

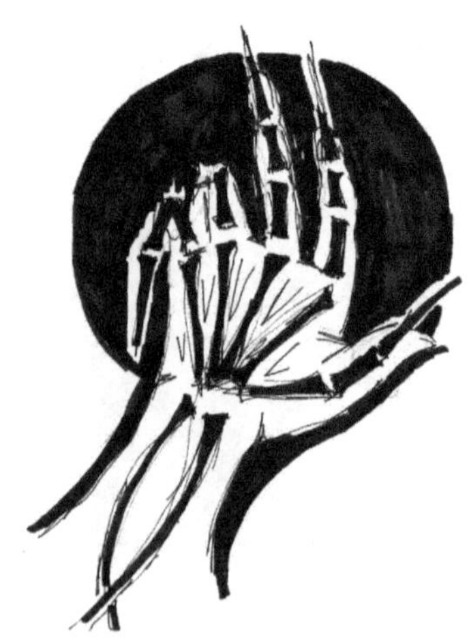

The Burden of Loss

How can something lost

Represent such a heavy burden?

The weight of your memory

The void of your absence

Overwhelms me

Some gaps are filled

Tools and council

Have increased my strength

But I almost happily admit

Complete recovery

Will never be achieved

Waiting in Breathlessness

Your inability to meet me there
To even consider the possibility
It is where I am
Where I choose to be

I have shown you the way
Enumerated the many benefits
But the barrier is high
Constructed by your own will

I don't judge your limitations
I don't fully comprehend your pain
But in conjunction also realise
If you want to be with me

The journey is yours to make
I was once where you are now
And I found my way to intimacy

Once I arrived
Nothing else compares
The risk is high
But the rewards are even more so

Join me when you can

I will be waiting

The Future of Hope

Will there come a day

When we shall be rejoined?

I would think not

But still, hope remains

Barriers exist - they are not trivial

But they are of your making

Not of my construction

It's not about my ability to forgive

It's that there is nothing to forgive

In the cool afternoon rain

I await your return

A Time for Growth

The devil is not sneaky, he announces himself.

Moving through and past the trauma takes a lot of work. If you have made it this far, you should be congratulated! My amateur definition of the growth period is a time that still represents dealing with pain but also demonstrable progress and the first glimpses of a better future and, dare I use the word, hope. Physiologically speaking, growth occurs when damaged tissue heals. A key concept is that if healing is allowed to proceed to completion, you inevitably come out stronger than your state prior to the thing that damaged you. Growth is also the stage of our journey where you get to utilize and master the tools that you have discovered or been given, so if you ever find yourself in a lesser state again, you can recall and use these gifts repeatedly.

The Joy of Sadness

The persistent ache

It's gone

It's back

Dammit. Will this torment ever cease?

I do not regret the pain though

For not everyone has loved so deeply

The Benefit of the Doubt

Memories are but

A narrative of the past

But now is not then!

Life and change are synonymous

I have changed enough

To give you the benefit

But I am certain of nothing

Influence

Would you have changed

Your behaviour, if you knew?

What a failure of self

Fantasise, love and pursue what you want!

Be strong and confident

Failure teaches

While regret consumes you

Observations of Reality

Humour eludes me

Not the simple mechanics

The misdirection, the double meanings

Pleasure response when your brain "gets it"

I mean, things just aren't that funny

My brain seems not to allow

The myth to endure

Laughing for even a moment

Reality on the surface is chilling

Dig even a little below the substrate

And discover only pain, hopelessness

I didn't choose to be here

It's just an observation of reality

The only true comedy left

The only authentic laughter that remains

Comes from the recognition

Of the utter futility of it all

Sonder

The unimaginable depths

In a spec of time

Incomprehensible complexity of information

A middle-aged man crosses a bridge

What stories he must contain

The depth of his love

The pain induced by his traumas

Even though his story is only partially told

Our deeply flawed methods of communication

Point to the clear impossibility

Of me ever even glimpsing

The depth and meaning of his reality

Multiply this by our daily connections

And again, by the ticks of a clock

I conclude as much as I wish to seek

As much as I desire to know others

I can never be even partially fulfilled

…

A woman eats breakfast alone

Here we go again!

Insights into Love

Love cannot be exchanged

It can only be gifted

If you are recording the transaction

It is not love you have

But some gross perversion

The hard truth becomes clear

However easy it may be to love another

Accepting love - especially undeserved

Remains a painful process

The dark fact is

My ability to accept love

Is limited by my shallow nature

To the extent I can love myself

This is a great sadness

Resolving this issue

Is of great importance

Nearing Conclusion

This might be the one

I have been here before

All roads lead to disappointment

But what else can I do?

The beat is primal

The dance, a fascination

Who am I

To challenge the ancestry?

My lineage was enough

Bred for success[9]

There is no fight left in me

I submit

The conclusion is still uncertain

It could still go either way

[9] This is not written from a place of vanity but a simple recognition of my evolutionary past and, by definition, their success against all odds that led to my existence. It's a fascinating thought when considered in the light of current science.

Each trial is independent

Past performance does not dictate

Future success - or failure

I don't so much roll the dice

As let them fall out of my hand

The Sharpening Stone

There exists a vast chasm

Between knowing a thing

And living that thing

A depth of understanding

That gives both power and weight

Momentum is thrust upon

The heavy stone wheel

That I imagine life to be

The gems of knowledge

Are often hidden

In dark crevices

Amongst dry piles of shit

Claw your way through it

Battle on!

For the surprise and the reward

Both exist and are worth it

Against the Flow

Society does not respect

My restless, erratic behaviours

Dreaming, seeking, searching, waiting

Why should these things be stifled?

I have not yet found my place

But as far as I know

I am still here

And I reject the notion

Of compromise, of normality

Anarchism is not a romantic dream

It is my concrete reality

And for this, I am chastised

Till my final breath

I will continue on my journey

So often, against the flow

Not in search of a destination

But for the joy of the dream

Hard Choices

How does one choose

Knowing simulations provide direction

But not the destination?

Fundamental paralysis ensues

As creatures of action

If one desires to persist

Simplicity must be valued

The accuracy of the forecast

Diminishes quickly with depth

Is this just another path

To the concept of survival bias?

Oddly having the knowledge

That we are simply stumbling blindly

May make the situation worse

So I am left with the dilemma

Of what action to take next?

One thing is for sure

My labour is wasted

The Gambler's Fallacy

The layers I have introduced

To protect me from harm

Also negate the pleasure

One day it just happened

The numbness, the paralysis

The shell is hard and thick now

Even to discover

This armour is of my design

I fear I may lack the knowledge

To break out of the cage

Furthermore, do I want to?

Sacrificing joy for the cessation of pain

Is an offer worthy of consideration

The alternative is a gamble

That has yet to pay off

A sunk cost fallacy?[10]

Throwing good money after bad

---

[10] Most often discussed in the context of economic theory, I find it equally applicable to a range of psychological and philosophical issues.

Choices

Acceptance of my lot

The hand I was dealt

The faulty logic in my bets

Will I find the answer?

On my inward quest?

To give up the struggle

Would provide such relief

The pain of losing you would end

But so would pass the memories

Even knowing the logical flaws

I continue the journey[11]

---

[11] With an academic background in mathematics, I often need to remind myself: "There is an in-between" and "The probabilities equal one." Both ideas are safeguards against our minds' ability to take things beyond the real, to the ultimate extremes.

The Conquering of Despair

What remains of fear?

I have gutted the monster

I still recognize the signs

And I respond

"Well done! Great effort!"

I am encompassed by peace

But a new darkness is spawned

As the fear died, so did motivation

The danger of seeing through the veil

Of contemplating the ultimate answers

Is the nothingness, the emptiness

To which all paths ultimately lead

To pick yourself up

To chance to go on

Takes enormous effort now

Misunderstood by those for whom

The battle still rages

Finish Lines

The ability to bear the pain, the hurt

Is lauded by the masses

But why should this be so?

Do I not envy those

Who simply collapse

Under the weight of it all?

For them, the journey is over

For them, their task is complete

Rest in the arms of another

I continue alone[12]

---

[12] A friend is not someone who wishes you well on a journey but says, "wake me up when we get there."

Opening Your Mind

But tomorrow always comes

At least in my experience

Be wise for tomorrow

Versus

Be in the now, enjoy today

"Choose!" she[13] yells

But the dichotomy is a false one

The journey for a better tomorrow

Is built by a series of nows

I was judging by a single standard

Now I see

It was so obvious

Mine was but one of many options

And more so

One of the least imaginative

---

[13] Who is "she"? I have no idea - but the voice at the time was clear and it was feminine.

Inner Flame

Reignite the flame

That once burned true and clear

Diminished by the lack of fuel

As your very life force

Is sucked out of the room

Scorch and char

Roast a new path with intensity

The best - or worst - experience of your life

Reflections of the same source

You can feel the heat

Energy builds and excites

Don't hesitate, feed it now!

Burning bright again

Your life focus becomes clear

You contemplate why

Did you ever leave this place?

You resolve not to judge too harshly

Returning was an active choice

Leaving was not

Your existence is now, here, the flame

I leave you burning bright again

Blaze long and hot

Consume the world

Leaning into It

What can be the advantage

Of paralysis as a state of being?

My very essence is locked

In a near-perfect description of nothingness

I smile and hide from others

A certain level of functionality

Is expected and even praised

But I know the truth

And I embrace it

For I have been here before

And know not to run from it

It is not fear

It is not anxiety

It is closer to a destination

Of true acceptance

Of deep central peace

Assured that the greatest potential

Has no meaning

A Time for Questioning

Question the obvious answer.

When dealing with and finding your way through trauma, I ask myself many questions. I find value in both asking the questions and attempting to derive answers - even if most of these pursuits are elusive to us - it is the exercise that matters.

I am a strong proponent of seeking professional mental help when required. Still, over time and through this ongoing healing process, I have been shocked at the number of times that satisfactory answers can be derived internally once the right question has been asked.

Finally, (alluded to in several poems found below), sometimes recognizing that it was the wrong question or a wrong "path" is just as valuable! Eliminating an incorrect answer (or question) can contain just as much value as finding an answer under certain circumstances.

Questioning the Wisdom of Being Present

Wise men say

There is only now

But what is the present?

If not a vantage point to observe

The potential futures

The distorted past

Worse still is knowing

The future is obscured

By a thick fog of ignorance

The past is a delusion

At best, an imperfect recollection

Maybe now is all we have

Is This the Way?

Is actively electing to enter the void

The place of deepest agony

A mandatory destination

On the journey of recovery?

I am unconvinced

Is it not more likely

That this blanket of numbness and paralysis

Is the emotional last defence

Of a mind in the throes of death?

Denying the complete

Brutal but honest

Truth of the thing?

Distant Hope

There still may be hope

A distant, almost imperceptible dream

For when I consider hate

I cannot fully penetrate the veil

My self-loathing is not yet absolute

I can only conclude

Even I perceive some redeeming yet unknown attribute

The question remains

Can such a tiny seed

Be discovered by another?

The Point

Lots of things are possible

But what are the pursuits?

I am adrift

In a sea of my thoughts

Oddly I have the energy

Resources abound

God knows I have the time

It is the destination

Or even a direction that I lack

Should my first goal be to define one?

Survival mode set aside

Abundance can be a curse

The only war to fight

The only territory unconquered

Is myself

Today Is the Greatest[14]

Today could be an earmarked day

One that spawns a chain of events

But consider

Does not every day contain that potential?

What hope that brings!

What adventures await!

"Be open and prepared," they say for success

I always focused on preparedness

But today, of all days

I embrace the open potential

Today could be the day

Yesterday could have been the day

Or just as likely tomorrow

A single grain of sand

Can lead to a deluge

Another enumerable reason

To focus on the small, the now

---

[14] Partial attribute (but not inspired by) to The Smashing Pumpkins' 1993 hit song "Today."

The Illusion of Choice

There is a stark difference

Between the inside and the external world

I assumed they were related

But now I see the truth

They are not

Is this the split?

The one that really matters?

Which do I pursue?

All things being equal

I choose the dream[15]

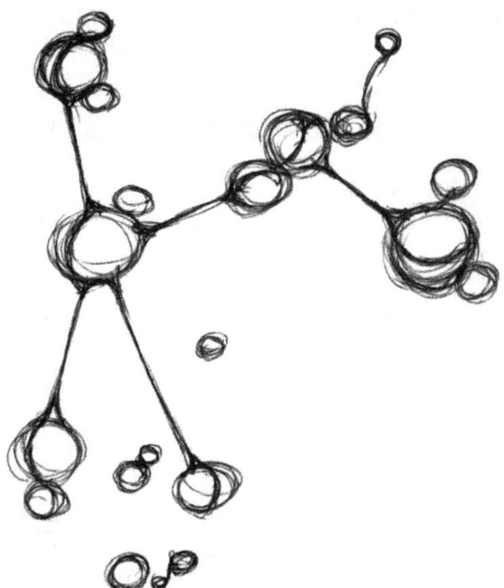

---

[15] It's not about "truth"; it is what people believe the "truth" is.

Discovery over Creation

The discovery of a truth

Potentially life-altering

Is only a matter of perception

It always was, it always will be

Let it enter you

Fill yourself with excitement

But never forget

It was you who changed

Not reality

Experience what is

Fall in love with the pursuit

It is not too late

Answers exist, and they are patient

Waiting, waiting for you

Digging Deeper

Consider the underlying causes

In all things

But don't delve too deep

You may not accept

The answers or lack thereof

In the lowest realms of reality

The surface level

Is often the least interesting

It also takes a greater effort

To familiarise yourself

With the infinite edge nodes

Probe deeper and deeper still

Gaining even some knowledge

Of the deeper substrate

Can have exponential benefits

Explanatory value multiplies

As answers are derived

Pull back the layers that shield you

From greater and more meaningful truths

Go forth, empowered one

Chaos and Order

Art exists

In the vast realm

Between order and chaos

In this way

Beauty really is in the eye of the beholder

I am partial to chaos

This comes as a revelation

While I tend toward order[16]

On any particular day

Is this the source of my inner struggle?

The thing that ever plagues me?

Is the pursuit of chaos the disease?

Or just as likely, the goal of order

The answer crystalizes quickly

Order, control - these are the myths

It is not so much that I prefer chaos

The truth is acceptance of it

---

[16] My chosen vocation is a Software Engineer, so as I lean more into my creative side, it truly was a revelation that I prefer chaos over the logical necessity of order as my work mandates.

Choice

An imperfection in my clothing

Shit on the carpet

Which is which?

It's just a contrast in perceptions

Who is fit to judge?

Fallacies abound and even multiply

We all exist in our own bubbles

We are all alone

What you elect to focus on

Is a personal choice

Embrace the freedom and choose wisely!

Pain, joy, good, evil

I say again - choose wisely!

Who Am I?

Where is joy?

What is joy?

I can give it away

It appears others have it

Possible? Yes

Practical? Yet to be determined

Something to be sought?

Or something to be discovered?

It would seem joy comes from within

But therein lies the problem

For I am not defined

Is It Enough?

I cannot at this moment

Justify my existence

There is some good

There is some bad

But taken on the whole?

The future is a series of potentialities

The darkness will surely carry the day

Is the glimmer of hope enough?

Hard Options

Unreciprocated love

Is a unique type of pain

Worse still

Is its enduring permanence

The time spent

The effort given

The only retort is indifference

Will confession lighten the soul?

Or be the death of self?

The Silent Response

The "null" response

Is even more powerful

Than I previously held

By leaving the question

Open so wildly

You eliminate such a small subset

Which by economic yield theory

Increases its value!

That is so weird

Sunlight is free

I am experiencing the deep

The void of the thin

Is often enough of an answer

Probabilities

What is the happiest moment of my life?

I do not have an immediate answer

Does that speak more to happiness?

Or my life in particular

As with most questions of merit

The answer most likely

Lies somewhere in between

False Dichotomies

I long for deep rest

It is an odd thing

To be unable to define

The source of this angst

It's all inside me

You would think it would be obvious

But the disparity remains

I am either whole, pure

Or damaged to an extreme degree

Is it possible I know the answers

But lack the courage to accept?

To execute my convictions?

Alternatively, in seeking change

Perhaps I have arrived

And this unfamiliar place

Is my new refuge

The calm that comes with knowing

Not seeking as a virtue

Future Trials

When the analysis is at its end

What I fear most is being

Held in the arms of another

Total surrender, total reliance

What is my purpose?

I define myself by what I give

Is my existence enough?

Although I am pretty confident it is invalid

The answer I fear is "no"

The only thing left to give

Is all of myself

In Search of Meaning

I want it all to mean something

The passion, pleasure, pain

I sense the end is near

Rushing towards me

And I still don't see the point

Am I the odd one out?

Or have I missed a universal truth?

Look at me seeking

Destination, purpose

Where none exist

It is a virtual pursuit

Our brains make it so

With no correlation

Not even analogous

To reality

Introspections

The ability to question yourself

Can be a superpower

But be on guard!

It can also be the source

Of your greatest weakness

Properly manipulated by those with malice

It can represent a path to serious self-doubt

And avoidance of obvious truths

Worse yet

Is the self-application

The toxic internal voices

The inner doubt can become vivid

The story is cruel

So on a regular basis

Reset this cycle

Before all sanity is lost

Izzy

Tell me of Isabelle

Is she hidden?

Beneath deep pain?

Or something else?

I could be wrong

I am open to that

I must ask

Dearest Isabelle[17]

---

[17] Izzy is one of my youngest Daughter's closest friends, and I should note in conclusion that I did ask her, and she is doing just fine!

A Time for Exploring

To consider that a single mind sitting in quiet contemplation can progress our understanding of reality is simply astonishing.

Psilocybin can be a wonderful aid when dealing with past, deep trauma. Opening up your mind and being present and conscious of the beauty that not only exists - but lies within you can be a powerful experience. Although my full dosing days may be behind me, I am a strong believer (backed by many modern studies) that there exists and continues to be longitudinal benefits for activating new and underused neural pathways in the brain.

Many of these poems are abstract in nature and may not be of taste to you. I enjoyed writing them and pondering them soberly after the fact - take what you will from them. I will accept insights into my mind, process, and healing from any source without judgement.

Mushroom Discoveries

The excitement of feeling

That first wave of freedom

Oh man, I did it this time!

Tear down the preconceived notions

Knowledge is but an illusion

Even more synapses are firing now

I can see something in the distance

Something fresh and new on the horizon

I have discovered a great truth

That truth is not a thing

And most importantly

It was the wrong question to begin with

The Nexus[18]

Now, the Nexus

The eye that brings forth focus

Introduces violations to past events

Defines potential futures

The awareness of such a Nexus

Is terrifying due to its power

And possibly the idea and concept

With the most explanatory value ever

---

[18] I "experienced" the nexus in a particularly deep session. The best sober explanation I can offer would be that it simultaneously represents the conjunction of all the past, present moments and potential futures.

Gone

For I have entered the place of laughter

I thought it was the last line

But it is the first

It does not need to be a dance song

To wear my cape[19]

Earlier I thought of the greatest vulgarity

I know it was great

Because 2nd place pales in comparison

I am spying on the dog now

I think I can outsmart him

Does he know about peripheral vision?

I shall investigate further

(The cape is wonderful, thank you)

He outsmarted me, the little devil!

Things are disconnecting

I am unsure if this is progress

Or retardation

---

[19] In reality, it is just a soft, warm blanket.

Uncertainty of Scope

I apologised

To a candlewick today

Have I finally arrived?

I assume there is more

There without the telling

"Now he's got it, by Jesus!"

There is legitimately more

Writing while high

It is not just a matter of degree

Of the "normal" filter mechanisms

I know you get it

Childlike Wonder

I am beyond the veil

Embrace it now

Cling to it

As a newborn to its mother

I can not be the first

To utter the words

Is it but a phrase?

The question minimises it so

Misdirections

It's tricky when it comes at you

Dressed as one thing

But really another

It is not a metaphor

It really is that!

Oh, who shall I tell[20]

The very exciting news

I got sidetracked

When I finally found the words

Everything is alive now

As it should be, as it always was

Be able to see, remember

Was shouted

As we faded away

---

[20] If you ever decided to experiment chemically in a safe environment, I recommend always doing so with some way to record your thoughts close at hand.

Reality in a Grain of Rice

Blindly scraping

In the dark

"I get it"

Trying to be mature and stuff

But in reality

It is hopeless

On all levels of reality

A single grain of rice

Less the expenditure of energy

The math is blinding[21]

Stop fighting, and rest

---

[21] Even though I was pretty intoxicated at the time of writing, I was still specifically contemplating Einstein's Theory of Relativity, specifically" $E^2 = (pc)^2 + (mc^2)^2$, actively contemplating the energy potential in a single grain of rice.

Wisdom of the Night Sky

So the guy says[22]:

"Any advantages of having poor eyesight?"

"Yeah," I say, "Looking at the stars"

"What do you mean?" He retorts

"They are all blurry and shit"

"Yeah," I say

"For every star you see, I see six"

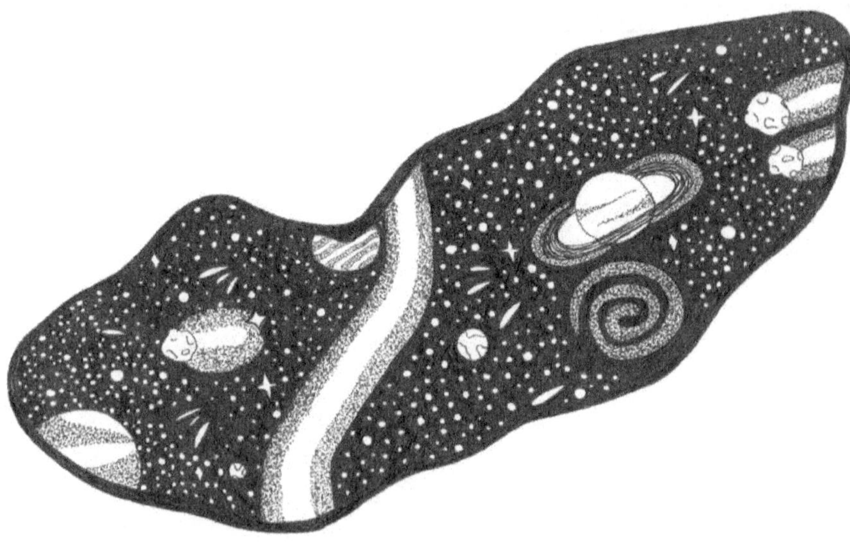

---

[22] Is this a poem? Arguably not, but when I had this "conversation" (I was alone walking my dog late in the evening), I still felt the insight was valuable enough to record and transmit to others.

Acceptance of Flow

It can be a cause of great angst

If one contemplates the nature and notion

Of growth and progress

All things are cyclic

We are but a leaf

Floating down a turbulent stream

We can no more fight the waves

Than we can outshine a dying star[23]

Let the illusion of control fall away

The shroud has been torn asunder

Focus solely on the motion

There is only now

There is only you

No matter how much you may rail against it

It is enough

For that is all there is

---

[23] Supernovas can release the energy of ten billion stars in their final moments.

Security

The empty blanket

Is a lover awaiting our return

I am not yet tired[24]

---

[24] The deeper meaning here in this short poem is my acceptance that I am, and even prefer not to be, in a relationship and that I rather curl up with a warm blanket at this time.

The Void Path

I'm not drunk enough for this

A glimpse of a place

A forbidden destination

Someone else is writing now[25]

Is this the void?

I am too far gone to acknowledge

It's gone now

It's terror but a fleeting moment

Return me to the void

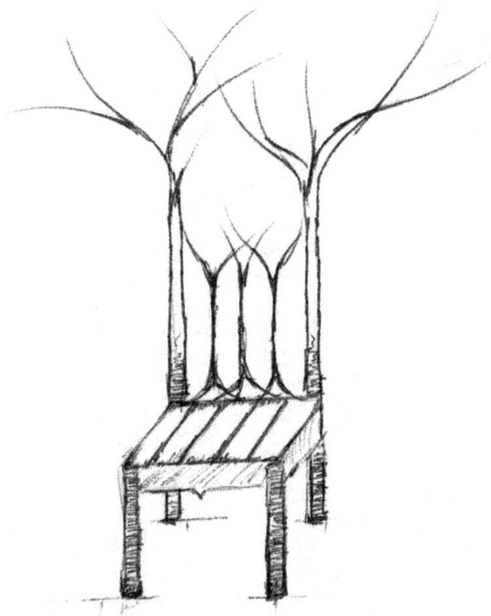

---

[25] This feeling of being outside of oneself is quite common; I have noted specifically that my handwriting is quite distinct from being in a sober state.

Tripp'n

Ply me with drugs

It is all "at once"

I catch a glimpse of that place

That is not just hidden

I forgot I was even looking for it

I am at ease now

I want to hold the moment

Be with me

For you are here

I am not in control

Or at least I shouldn't be

Perspectives

The fields are wasted

Unappreciated by the young

Only observed by the old

If you only fucking knew

How evidently beautiful you are!

It should cause great pain

The potent and simple truth of it all

But I am at the stage of laughter[26]

---

[26] The more I pursue mindfulness, the more often my reaction to various situations is laughter.

Water Dance

I put it on repeat

I remember now

I thank my past self

I sell the virtues

To my future being

I think even the water dances now

But consider - what other option -

Does water have another state?

Water is over there

The bass line has clarified

A new voice enters

Shadowing the star

Why would you elect

To not be at peace?

I get to fill the space

I am in control

Of what enters

I think I will try something new

Spacetime

Cones of light

Penetrating the infinite yet bounded

Perpendicular to causal experience

The gravity well has you[27]

It's not that you can't get out

But the past you can not revisit

Only in your mind

And even then

A fading and inaccurate memory

---

[27] I think a lot about the physical experience and physics of falling into a black hole. Time becoming perpendicular to our normal perception of the dimension, as an example in this instance, is just one of the fascinating effects to contemplate.

Voices in My Head

A distant chanting

Begins to sound clear

So many voices!

Yet I am alone

Although I am of one mind

My inner dialogue remains distinct

Progress is achieved

Through virtual mental means

It's not about winning a debate

What would that even mean?

The only pursuit is truth

For what other purpose

Should we give voice?

Re-Learning

Is defect now

But a marketing campaign?

Have they finally rediscovered

That imperfection is beauty?

Listen to the subtle ones

The ones way below

The layers of beauty

Run ever so deep

I feel like I have known this before

That this is re-learning

Something of friction

To selectively forget

Is a gift only granted to gods

A Time for Healing

A single friend can be a light in the darkness.

Healing, or at least the minimization of pain, does come with time, even though it may not seem like progress is being made over shorter intervals. Healing can be accelerated through authentic and meaningful self-reflection. I encourage you to seek out the tools - and master them - if you are ready to seek wholeness again.

In my experience, I would also note that healing tends to come in layers. Once one past or present difficulty is understood and dealt with, it opens up the door for you to more clearly see that there is another challenge that lies ahead. I feel confident after cycling through this a number of times now that this part of the journey does not ever conclude.

Expanding Boundaries

Without form or focus

I let my mind wander

Ceding control to my creative self

Protected and so deeply hidden away

On this journey inwards

Where shall I go next?

One thing is for certain

There are no incorrect destinations

Abstractions merge with the concrete

In new and often hilarious ways

Stretching the boundaries of the possible

Edging towards the infinite

There is always more to know

The undiscovered a vast shadowy plane

I will continue my journey

Recognizing the illusion of nearing completeness

Is but my first step of many

Infinite Opportunities

A beautiful flow of phrase

Deeply intimate and kind words to a stranger

Don't hold back

Never restrain

As paralleled with love

These are not finite resources

Give without the expectation of reciprocity

Define the world by example

Move forward without fear

Knowing the end is nigh[28]

Becomes part of the solution

Step forward with renewed confidence

Rest, sleep in peace

---

[28] The fifth stage in the grieving process.

Intervals

Get up, you fool!

It is your only task

You failed - so fucking what?

"You" are not a failure

The year, month, weekday

Even the hour and minute are not failures

Only the moment was a failure

And it has passed!

Delegate it to history, to memory

Fail short and live again

The same applies to success

Fighting Against Shame

The bar is getting lower

Thresholds eaten away

Arbitrary limits

Why not experience

We are all trying

Accept me for what I am

Imperfect, defective

Honesty in choice

Deep Roots

The root structures

Of even the greatest trees

Are wide but not deep

The tendril of depth is rare

Our lives are of such a nature

Allow your mind to be broad

Allow a vast array of connections

But choose wisely

When you contemplate things of great meaning

Those things of depth

Alone and in the dark

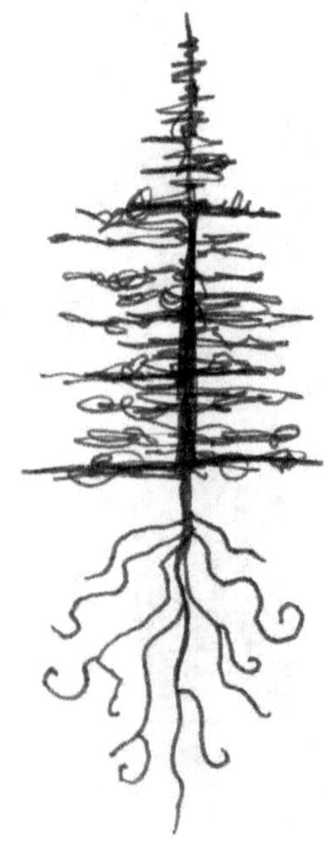

The Moonlit Walk

I have trodden the fields

In the dead of night

The soft ground under my feet

You may deny it

But you were with me

I held your hand

As we walked in silence

The moonlight being our guide

Wandering agendaless

We found peace

I do not fear being alone

But together, I recognize

We are both finally whole

Now Is the Time

"Dance Motherfucker"
Wiser words may never have been spoken
Life is lived in the moment
It is not something that happens
Life is something you do!

Seize the opportunities as they arise
If none are present, manufacture them!
Bored with creation? Imagine!
Participate in something novel every day

Cry for joy at the sight of loved ones
And tell them often how you feel
When righteous rage builds
Feel it all, scream aloud when you must

Guilt and shame
Are burdens you need not bear
Step away - nay - run from negativity
Pursue justice and equality in all things
Know your core, and live by it

Rewards come in many forms
Accept them when they present
Explode with light, rupture with love
Dive ever deeper into empathy
Contemplate mortality daily

Do all the things unfinished
Say all the things unsaid
Now dance with a lightened heart
You glorious, beautiful Motherfucker!

Beauty in Scope

There is a point too far

Going beyond loses meaning

Some insights require the microscope

Others mandate the macroscope

The virtual realm is another tier

The general observation

Is to limit the desired scope

Like a negative determinant

At some scales

The answers become nonsensical

Apply this to beauty

Apply this to song

When you discover the beauty of the thing

Look no further

First Sight

The excitement of seeing

A beautiful stranger

Is explained simply by hope

In a flash, a speck of time

We compress a lifetime of dreams

Of joy and happiness

Into that first blip

As we age, as we fail

We are tempered

By additional chapters

In our evolving epic saga

Inevitable pain

Inevitable sorrow

Inevitable demise

But these are the latter chapters of our story

The first moment

Remains sheer bliss

No Limits

I have discovered a new way of being

It is neither original nor unique

Flowing, with a lack of permanence

It is not about a destination

I clash against rigidity

Purpose is a myth

Accept the external

As a series of fleeting, momentary gifts

Consume them for what they are

And then let them pass through you

Existence is fleeting

How ever more so are individual perceptions?

Be here with me

Be here now

It is all we ever had, ever will have

Boundless is my love for you

I seek nothing more

Accelerating Towards the End

Our advanced civilization

Is accelerating toward destruction

Local gains

Offset by global catastrophes

The pursuit of wealth

Is an obvious blunder

Time is the finite resource

What is the end game now?

Even our limited choices

Are mere delusion

Our race to extinction

Was inevitable from the start

With what little time remains

Be present, actively grateful

Soberly reflect on the small

The daily, intimate transactions

Seek to manifest love

Let others discover it in you

In this dying world

The Weight of Struggle

We push, and we push

We educate ourselves in new techniques

We solicit external advice

We construct and master new tools

To ever increase our leverage

But alas, this immovable object

Remains intact, unshaken, unmoved

Respite only comes

Through the chance revelation

That the battle is with ourselves

You cannot affect the box from within

Your efforts are not in vain

For there is only one path

You only achieve victory

When you give up the fight

Life Song

The sun has set

Was joy found on this day?

Is it a place? A time? An event?

Discovered or manufactured?

One's perspective must play a role

The more centred I become

The more laughter is the answer

Choose to pluck the memory

That guides you to a smile

Consider your mental focus

That which consumes you the most

The answer should be obvious

If it is not, reflect and return

In this, I do not only find joy

I become it, I exist in it

Yes, I am happy

My compass tells me so

Getting to the Core

Conciseness of form

Brevity in words

Misinterpreted by many

As a lack of intelligence

But in reality

An active choice to communicate

Minimized actions in a similar vein

Represent true authenticity

Caring is amplified, not minimized

Strip the world down

Consciously derive priorities

And abide with kindness and flexibility

This is true form

Often not respected by the masses

The sheer deep irony

Carries no weight

Discussion Around the Unknown

The guy asks me

"Is it a logical OR choice?"

"I don't know," I say bluntly, honestly

"Fuck" he retorts

"Yeah, I know man, I get it," I soothe

Not even knowing the question

Feels weird at first

But pretty quickly

You are at home

You are at peace

The Sober Dance

Can I really dance sober?

As I increase the volume

I travel deeper inside

My goal is the high

Without the artificial accelerants

They have been a gift

But only in helping me discover

What was always present

Close your eyes, focus on breathing

The song repeats, louder still

The powerful bass line rumbles

It should be felt, not heard

I yearn for a breakthrough

But logic is the hindrance

Not the answer

Increase the volume again

And dance!

Ignorance in Death[29]

How sad I feel for you

You have pretended for so long

Reality is lost to you

Misdirection, reflection and denial

These are the tools of the lost

The hardening of your mind

Has led to a hardening of your heart

All that remains to you

Are mythos and fable

One last hope remains

That your mythology lasts till the end

For if you ever wake to reality

And catch a glimpse of what has been lost

I fear the pain would be too great

So I pray you embrace your slumber

It is my final kindness to you

---

[29] This writing could have fit in a number of different chapters, but ultimately it is about kindness and forgiveness in the face of deep trauma and hurt. So from my perspective, it is optimally associated with healing.

A Time for Hope

A fallen petal in the morning light is everything it needs to be; it is complete.

After a great deal of work and effort, there is a possibility that, mixed with the passage of time - and I wish it dearly for you - of discovering hope anew.

In my long journey through trauma and questioning, love and reflection, there were times I was not certain any hope remained, but the investment was worth it and did pay off for me, and I believe it can for you as well.

Even though we have arrived at the final chapter of this book and the conclusion of this small part of my journey, the complete and unknown trek has not reached its final destination. One gem of wisdom I have learned recently and am still coming to terms with is this: Mental health cycles, this is natural and expected. If you find yourself having a bad day, week, month or even a year - remember that this is just part of a cycle and that things will inevitably improve naturally and often without any concerted effort.

Springtime Sunrise

Oh, how I long for

The season of full bloom

Life returns in all its glory

Lost hope transforms into potential

Options and alternatives expand

Darkness fades

Replaced by light and love

The sunlight has new meaning

Warming me from the inside first

How odd that I forget

These feelings of hope

All seemed lost

But a short time ago

The scent of spring flowers

Renews me once more

The Empty Vessel

Should I give thanks

For this inability to feel?

Have I reached a destination

Only to find it wanting?

Or have the wounds inflicted

Sliced clear through the nerves

Perhaps I have cried my last tears

The pain of your absence

Delegated to an intellectual exercise

Joy, hope and love

All equally elusive

I am but an empty shell

Perhaps this is a healthy step

On the journey to be a person again

For now, I get to choose

To exert full control

Over how to fill this vessel

Tiny Steps

A soft drizzle tingles

The dampness puddles

The deluge is inevitable!

We so often desire the outcomes

Without understanding the sheer simplicity

Of a granular series of tiny motions

Small, earnest, focused efforts

Take heart, the rewards will come!

Focus on the small, the minor things

Morphing imperceptibly slow over time

To a grand design and purpose

Awake with awe in the morning calm

Recognizing how far you have journeyed

Now you can know, demonstrate with confidence

The simplicity of the process

While still fully engaged

With the work, the road ahead

Journey forth and grow!

Expended strength returns in time

Multiplied manyfold

The Value of Contemplation

Another day has ended

Have I done the best I can?

To be strong tomorrow

We must work hard today

Contemplate the choices of the day

Correct the mistakes where you can

Try not to duplicate the ones you can't

Be present and aware

Your destination requires a planned route

And then a long multitude of steps

If you have no direction in mind

Your existence will be as a spinning top

Consider for a long time in deep contemplation

What you wish your priorities to be

Know them, live them, become them

Decisions will become so obvious

In the light of such knowledge

In the illumination of such self-reflection

Be generous in forgiveness

First and foremost, to yourself

Grow in wisdom daily - or not -

For me, I choose a life of meaning

New Visions

The scale and scope of life

Our daily routines tend to

Normalise our perceptions

Presented with new boundaries

An exaggerated sense of height and depth

Shattering beauty and awe

A reminder of true geological time

I reflect on what I may be missing

What defines normal to me

Be open to that bird song

Perhaps the most beautiful and intricate

Collection of tones and pulses I have ever heard!

Imagine the depths of a soul

In the most mundane of daily interactions

Beyond this, I recognize the truth

That even as I allow my limits to expand

There is still a long, long way to go

The Epic Journey

To climb a great mountain
Has more to do with perseverance
Than skill or strength

False starts are not only acceptable
They are expected
Some paths start easy and get hard
Others offer challenge and ease with time

For one can not envision
The scope, the scale, the contours
Of the vast journey ahead
You will stumble, you will fall, you will fail

Pick yourself up and continue onward!
If you are ever so lucky
And find yourself not alone
Then take the hand as it is offered to you
Lean on those who trek with you
Sharing the joys and the trials
Make the passage a sweeter place

Here is the final trick

There is no summit!

Only the journey exists

But it is worth the efforts

The views as one ascends

Justify each agonizing step

Depth of Mindfulness

Vastness of the great ocean

Quiet solitude in a single breath

Contrast and search for a depth of meaning

Dive deep into the abyss

Of the water, of your soul!

Observe the tendrils of life

That bind us together, that make us whole

Pluck at a random chord

And marvel at the ensuing complexities

Sensate feelings without regret

Growth may just be the transition

From being formed by others

To the awareness followed by acceptance

That we are not to be discovered

But rather to be formed

Each and every day anew

Finally, controlling the development process

Truly conscious, in each and every moment

We arrive again

At the depths of the ocean

The glorious present exhale

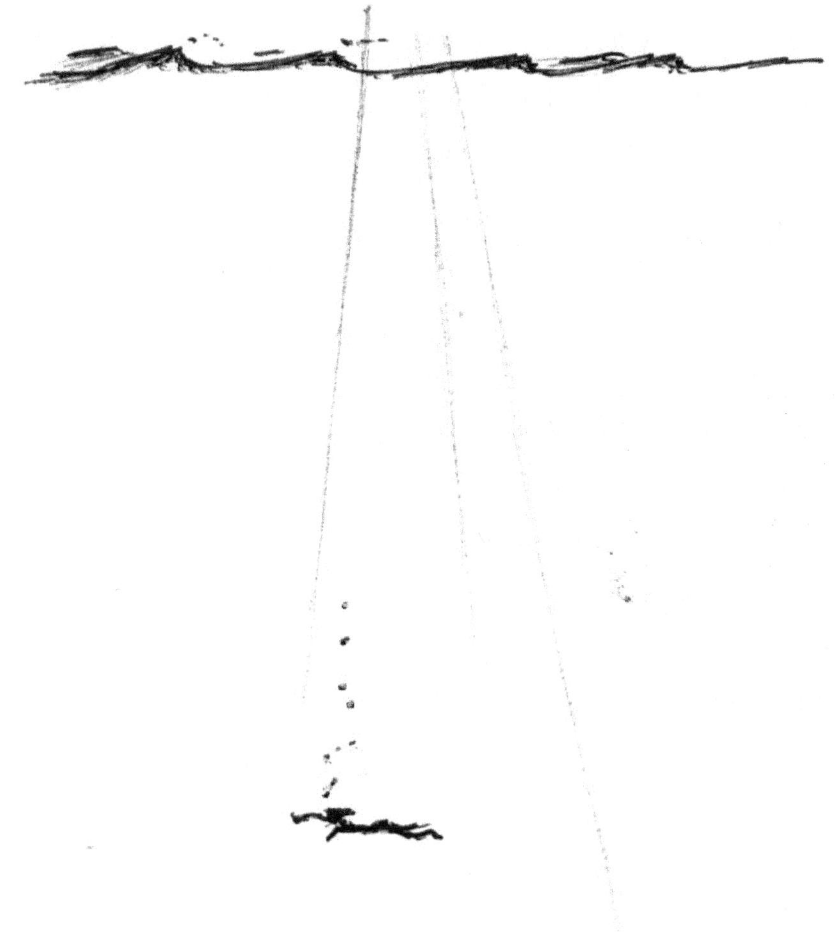

Happy Birthday

Listen now

Listen deeply and clearly

I see your potential as

Almost without limit

Your very presence in a room

Is a natural source of radiance

I draw energy from your hope

Your outer beauty shines!

Your inner beauty is glorious!

Don't squander these rare gifts

When lesser people bring you down

See through the vitriol of life

Pierce through the veil of pain

To be cared for by you

To even be considered by you

Causes giants to weep with joy

You are the prize

It will always be a privilege

To be loved by you

And love you in return

The Canvas

I slept to the sound of a river

Carving its path through a mountain ravine

My soul is etched with such scars

Some routes dried long ago

Others still raging, their final depths unfathomed

Still, it is all a beauty

I do not carry shame

I do not live in regret

Without the valleys

We would not have the mountain peaks!

The erosion, the evolution

Tied to an incomprehensible network

Reminds me of a simple fact:

I am alive, I am here, I exist

The final landscape of my life

The beautiful portrait being arranged

Is far from complete

The paint will always be wet

Dried only when the artist

Requires a final rest

Springtime Gifts

Life essence returns once more

Even though the yearly cycle is constant

I still feel gratitude, amazement and joy

In each new bud, a seed of beautiful potential grows

The staggered release of beauty and bloom

Is a gratitude worth noting on its own

For delivered all at once could overwhelm me

The sunlight and the warmth appear

The vibrant colours feed my will to go on

Sweet smells are as virgins to my senses

Perhaps another gift derived

Is that is merely a season

This overload as a constant may numb the magnitude

Appreciation of such small things should be retained

And consciously acknowledged and valued

Another observation worth noting

Is the value of foliage

The mystery returns once again

To the skittering creatures of the land

Sight too deep stifles the imagination

Not knowing what is beyond

Is so often an overlooked gift

I accept all these things

I harken them to be part of me

And am better for it

In Pursuit of the Real

I only have patience for the real

The intimate, the heartbreak

What generally is accepted as of importance

Is so often utter nonsense

A constant drivel of shit

Put in the effort!

Reset your perspectives

And gain great strength

Don't waste my time

But more importantly,

Don't waste your own

For those who hear me now

It fills me with great joy

To know I am not alone

I look forward to knowing you

"Knowing you" in the deepest real sense

Acceptance is not compliance

My empathy extends so deep

I don't know you,

But I already love you

Now Is the Time

What can I do to help?

What hope can people cling to?

In these final days

Each breath is a gift

Give thanks to everyone!

Know it - lean into it - fully experience it

Seek beauty and serenity

Actively pursue acceptance and calm

Say out loud the things typically unsaid

Step out of yourself

And find the beauty once again

In the here, the now, the essence of everything

Be centred, calm and confident

On this, the final leg of the journey

For not everyone will find

The purity of this love

Love's Eternal Hope

To my unknown lover

Before I knew you

You were in my thoughts

I have a rich history

I do not wish to forget

But nothing compares to you

I have collected a lot of pieces

But you are the thing

That adds context to it all

My frozen isolation

Has been thawed by your beauty

Prior to you, I existed

Now that you are with me

I finally live

Even though we found each other late

And our time together is less than desired

The quality will make up for it all

Where are you, my love?

Back on the Road

I have arrived

At my planned destination

Only to discover

That it was the journey I sought

Choosing a new direction

Getting back on the road

Feels different now

It is no longer a race

For there are no winners

I travel alone now

Others pass me by

But I am at peace once again

My journey has just begun

Early Morning Reflections

The crisp leaf skitters

Dances across the frozen earth

Even apart from its mother tree

Its life cycle is not yet complete

Many tasks lie unfinished!

Lending its beautiful flow of form

To an otherwise dreary morning

Inspiring a bit of undirected prose

Its vanishingly small mass

Amplified manyfold by the weight of thought

Appreciate the very tiny things

Enjoy the mystery

Of where the seeds of joy take root

Oh tiny friend

No comprehension of spheres of influence

Yet so connected we have become

I dare say intimately

I feel privileged to have witnessed

An honour to be a part of

The greatest of shared small joys

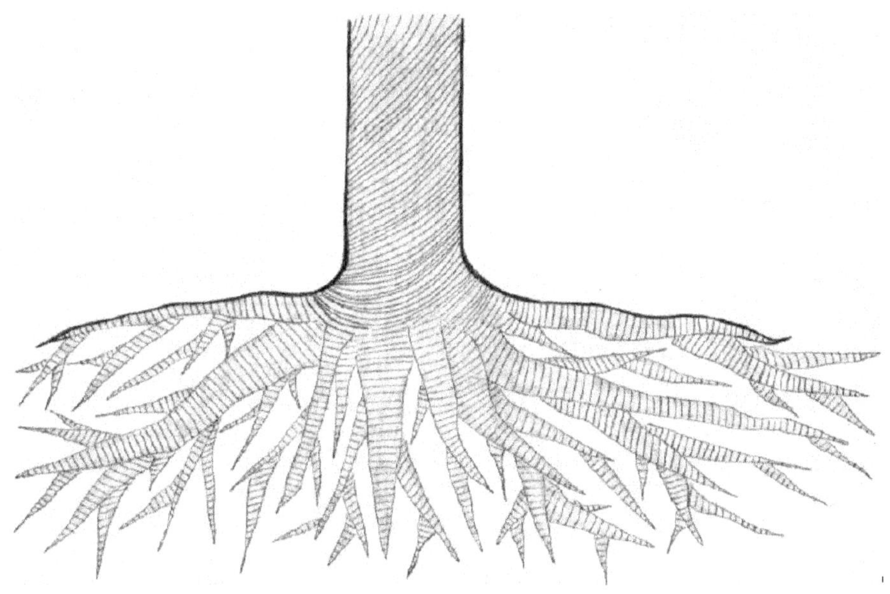

The Waitress

The power of laughter
To make a lasting impression
A positive contribution
To an otherwise bleak reality

A causal change is started
Its effects permeate like wildfire
Don't ever underestimate
What your joy can do for others

Positive lasting memories
Are not bound by time or space
Neither class, ethnicity or gender
But grow and thrive as only hope can

What stories have been told
What myths contrived and shared
Your tiny gift of laughter
Has grown with time and love

In an unexpected twist of destiny

The recipient of joy transforms into a source

You are now fed by your own creation

Does joy inevitably return?

In the end

The conclusion is clear

Be the joy as often as you can

Let the seeds of laughter take root

String Quartet

The music begins to play
Emotion overwhelms me
Tears flow without constraint
I know not why I cry

Is it from pain?
Is it from loss?
Perhaps from joy?

All I know is
The emotion springs forth from deep inside me
Spilling forth as the quartet plays
As the melody consumes me
So do the emotions

The beauty is within me
How did I not see it before?
So close to the surface
How long have I existed with such a capacity?
While still in complete ignorance

It is in me, it is in you

The beauty I assumed was external

Resides in completeness within

The voice that screams I am worthless

Is still alive and well

But now, as with conversing tones

A new voice has joined the chorus

It is my voice

Hidden for so long

It now rings clear, strong and proud

Freedom

I am not trapped

I just am where I am

Why should an alternate destination

Be so desired?

What awaits me there

That I can not experience here?

Hypothetically, this seems obviously true

The mind represents a most powerful mechanism

But I also speak of perceived reality

What depth of time would it take

What degree of intellectual rigour

Could lead one to the ignorance

Of claiming knowledge - let alone understanding -

The nature of one's current position?

Even for a moment of time

This is the real, the now

Versus the potential, untold future

I have so far to travel

Without ever taking another step